Persuasions

DOUGLAS WILSON

MOSCOW, IDAHO

Douglas J. Wilson, *Persuasions*

© 1989 by Douglas J. Wilson. Published by Canon Press, P.O. Box 8741, Moscow, ID 83843

01 00 99   9 8 7 6 5 4 3

Cover design by Paige Atwood Design, Moscow, ID

Printed in the United States of America.

ISBN: 885767-29-3

This book is dedicated to
my father and mother, who have been
used by God to turn many away from the Abyss.

Persuasions

Table of Contents

The Road 7
Randy — Immorality 9
John — Antinomianism..................... 15
Janice — Feminism 21
Jack — Agnosticism....................... 29
Rev. Howe — Empty Scholarship.............. 35
Mark — Atheism 41
Robert — Election 47
Jim and Sarah — Marriage 53
Dorothy — Hypocrisy in the Church........... 61
Bill — Salvation and Sanctification 67
Miriam — Pantheism...................... 75
Paul — Evolution........................ 81
Michael — Roman Catholicism 89

There was only one Road in that region, but like all roads, it ran in two directions. In one direction, it ran eastwards up a gradual incline, and ended at the City. In the other, the end of the Road was the Abyss.

In some places, the two destinations were obvious; in others, where the Road wound down through some canyons in the badlands, the truth was less obvious. Still, it was impossible for anyone to travel for any length of time on this Road without coming to some realization of his basic direction.

Nevertheless, those who were headed to the Abyss were also headed downhill, and preferred that to the strenuous alternative. There were many who therefore chose to ignore the unpleasant truth. The Master of the City had posted roadsigns warning of the danger, but roadsigns could be ignored as well.

The Master therefore instructed his servants, who were on their way to his City, to do their best to persuade these travelers to reverse direction. Some of them, discovering that the Master had given them some ability in this, became quite effective in the endeavor.

This is the story of one such individual. As he traveled to the City, he encountered many who wanted to go the other way, for many reasons. From long experience, he found himself answering them according to their particular objections. I have gathered here some of the conversations, in the hope that others who are traveling to the City may make some use of them.

Randy

As I dreamed, I saw a man named Evangelist turn and look down a road. In the distance, a figure was approaching. He was certainly taking his time.

As he walked up, Evangelist greeted him cordially and they began to talk. They engaged in what appeared to be small talk for a few moments, and I learned that the man's name was Randy.

"Where are you going?" asked Evangelist.

"Oh, nowhere in particular. I just go where the women are."

"And why is that?"

The young man laughed, and his laugh seemed to be full of both mockery and shame. "What do you mean why? Everyone needs a little now and then."

Evangelist answered him gravely. "Are you speaking of fornication?"

"Fornication? You make it sound like a disease! Sex is a normal and healthy thing."

Evangelist replied, "To be sure, sex is normal and healthy. But I wasn't talking about sex, I was talking about fornication."

Randy laughed again. "And what's the difference?"

"Fornication occurs when there is no marriage commitment. Adultery occurs when a marriage commitment is violated. But sexual activity within the boundary of marriage is something that God honors."

"God! God! You're not religious, are you? What does God have to do with sex?"

"He invented it. That's like asking what Thomas Edison has to do with light bulbs."

"What do you mean?"

"I mean that God is the one who designed sex in the first place."

"Then why do you Christians have such a thing about sex? You're always saying who should be sleeping with whom and who shouldn't."

Evangelist replied, "It is a common misconception that opposition to the perversion of a thing is the same as opposition to the thing itself. But of course the idea is absurd."

"How is it absurd?" Randy asked.

"If someone wanted to draw a mustache on the Mona Lisa, would that be an act of vandalism?"

"Of course it would."

"If you had the opportunity to stop such an act, would you?"

"Certainly."

"Would you step in as a friend of art or as an enemy of it?"

"As a friend."

"But suppose the vandal reviled you as an enemy of all that is beautiful. How would you answer him?"

"I would not need to answer him. The accusation is absurd."

"Exactly so. Absurd is the right word. And if you have understood the argument, you will stop accusing Christians of being the enemy of the thing they desire to protect. Sexual immorality destroys a very great gift of God. Immorality is vandalism."

Randy retorted, "If that is so, then why are you Christians so hush-hush about the whole subject? If you think it is so wonderful, why don't you talk about it more?"

"It is clear you don't know very many Christians."

Randy paused for a moment, considering the point. Evangelist's argument may have made some sense to him, because he tried to take the offensive again.

"Look, you religious types are all alike. You look down your noses at people having a good time, and you're envious. You wish you could get a little action. But you can't because of all your rules. So you cram your rules down our throats."

Evangelist smiled and slowly shook his head. "I will not defend the rules; they are not mine to defend, they are God's. He will apply and defend them adequately enough. As to your accusation of envy, I have only one thing to say. If I see a 400-pound man on the street, I do not envy him all the additional pleasure he has had at the dinner table. Nor do I envy you your time in bed."

Randy stepped back several paces, looking confused. He was not getting the best of the exchange, and he was not sure why. He usually had a good deal of fun with Christians.

"I can't imagine anything more boring than what you say God requires. Making love to only one woman for life. God! That's like buying one record and taking it home and playing it over and over and over again."

"I'm afraid your analogy is a faulty one. It is not like buying one record, it is like buying one instrument and learning how to play it. If you are committed, boredom is not a danger."

Randy's laughter was increasingly nervous, and he had a hunted expression.

"I just couldn't live like you do. I want to spend my time around pretty women."

This time it was Evangelist's turn to laugh, but there was no mockery in it. "Then why do you spend time with women who are not? My wife, Compassion, is a beautiful woman, and her beauty begins on the inside. I have never been ashamed of her. I would be very ashamed indeed to be involved with a woman who was willing to be used as a thing."

By this time Randy looked very uncomfortable. He was looking at the ground, and he started to move away.

"I really need to be going," he said.

Evangelist put a gentle hand on his arm.

"Before you go, may I ask you one question?"

"Go ahead."

"You have a habit, and that habit has enslaved you to your lusts. So much is understandable. But why do you boast in the vice?"

Randy looked at Evangelist for a moment. He was obviously thinking hard.

"If I come back here later, will you be here?"

"If God is willing."

"You say that I am a slave. Do you know how slaves can be set free?"

"I do."

"I need some time to think. I may be back."

With that, Randy turned and slowly resumed his walk down the road. It was clear that, for the first time in many years, a completely different kind of desire had come over him.

John

After a few minutes, I could make out an approaching figure in the distance. As he came nearer, it was obvious that he carried himself with confidence. He greeted Evangelist cheerfully. "Good morning, sir. How are you?"

"I am well, thank you," replied Evangelist. "And yourself?"

"Couldn't be better. It is such a beautiful day for travel. Will you join me on my journey? A companion to converse with would be a pleasure. My name is John." He extended his hand and Evangelist took it.

Evangelist introduced himself, but then went on to say, "I am afraid that I cannot come with you."

"And why is that?"

"I have no wish to go where you are going," answered Evangelist. "I must warn you that this road leads to the Abyss."

At this remark, John broke into merry peals of laughter. "My dear friend, I feel you have gotten your directions quite confused! I am going to the City. Behind me is the Abyss. You will be quite safe to travel with me."

"What assurance do you have of your direction?"

"Assurance?" asked John, surprised. "The very best! Many miles back, I met a man—he was dressed as you are—who gave me my instructions. He said that if I followed them carefully, I would find myself, in due time, at the gates of the City. He said I would be gladly accepted."

"And what were these instructions?"

"Actually, they have not been that difficult, although I am told that some have trouble with them. I was baptized, and have attended church faithfully. I have also given money regularly, and have tried to be a good man."

"But are you sure your teacher was correct?" said Evangelist. "What was his name?"

"He did not give me his name. But I am sure he spoke the truth. He showed me these things in his Bible. Doesn't the Bible speak of baptism? Aren't we told to gather together?"

"I am not as concerned with what he told you as with what he did not."

"What do you mean?" asked John.

Evangelist replied, "The Bible speaks of the things you mention. But there is more. Far more." Saying this, Evangelist took out a small black Bible, and opened it. He then began to turn pages slowly, carefully reading a list of requirements. He was very quiet and methodical. "Do not commit adultery." "Anyone who looks at a woman lustfully has already committed adultery with her in his heart." "Do not murder." "Anyone who is angry with his brother will be subject to judgment." This went on for about ten minutes. As he spoke, he looked very industrious—like a man loading a truck. During this time, John was looking increasingly distressed. His earlier confident attitude was fading. He looked like he was under some kind of a heavy weight.

"My teacher didn't explain it this way. He said that if I was sincere, and that if I did more good than bad, I would be accepted."

"Did he quote the passage to you that says 'faith without works is dead?'"

"Yes, that is the passage. That is where he started."

"But in that same place, the author also says that anyone who breaks the law at just one point is guilty of breaking all of it. To break one law is to break all laws."

"How is that?"

"Many think that the law of God is like a frame full of small window panes. They think that if they can get through life without breaking most of them, they will be all right."

"That's right, isn't it? After all, there are commands I haven't broken."

"No, I'm afraid not. This passage indicates that the law of God is more like one large plate glass window. And it doesn't matter if the hole is in the upper left hand corner, the lower right hand corner, or right in the middle. The window is still broken."

There was a panicked look in John's eyes, and his shoulders were stooped. He was breathing with some difficulty. Evangelist stepped back. "Now you are all set. When you get to the City, you will have to prove to them that you have kept all these requirements. They will then receive you gladly."

"This isn't realistic!" John moaned. "Do you expect me to crawl there on my knees? I can't keep all these requirements!"

"But these requirements are in the Bible, just like the ones you mentioned earlier. You have little time to waste. You had better get started."

At this, Evangelist stood aside to let John continue his journey. He started to walk off at a snail's pace—still toward the Abyss. A moment later, he turned back.

"Nobody can do this!"

Evangelist nodded. "That is correct."

"You are telling me that the City will be empty. No one will live there."

"No, that is not right. The City will be full."

John shook his head. "You're not making any sense to me. How can a City be full of men who can't get to it?"

"What a man cannot do may still be done for him."

John shook his head again. "Just what I needed. A guide who talks in riddles!" He then turned, and walked slowly down the road. Evangelist smiled briefly. It was clear he expected to see John again. Shortly.

Janice

In my dream, I saw a solitary figure walking quickly down the road toward us. I could see it was a woman.

As she came near, Evangelist smiled and greeted her. He extended a small book to her, which she declined as she hurried by.

Evangelist looked around at her. "Are you sure you don't want to talk about it?"

She looked over her shoulder.

"Yes, I'm sure."

"Perhaps that's wise."

The woman, whose name was Janice, whirled in her tracks.

"What did you mean by that?"

"I simply meant that when people hear truth before they are ready for it, it hardens them."

Janice glared at Evangelist. She thought for a moment, and then apparently changed her mind. She walked slowly back toward us.

"Truth, eh? You believe in absolute truth?"

"Certainly."

"I thought as much. The trouble with you Christians is that you are just like the Nazis or any other group that claims to have a corner on 'absolute truth.' You are so cocksure that your truth is the only truth, you fill the earth with your disputes. You make me sick." At this Janice turned to go.

"Excuse me a minute. You have overlooked something," Evangelist said.

"And what is that?"

"If there are no absolute standards, then why should the Nazis have been resisted? How do you know they were wrong?"

"Of course they were wrong. They murdered millions of people."

"You're beginning to sound like an absolutist. Why is it wrong to murder millions of people?"

Janice stared at Evangelist as if he was a madman.

"You're not saying they were right, are you?"

"Certainly not. But I'm able to say they were wrong because I believe God has revealed his absolutes to man. I can resist the Nazis because I believe truth to be absolute. How do you say they are wrong?" Janice looked at Evangelist, at a loss for words. Evangelist started up the conversation again.

"Look, the Nazis are a good illustration from history, but we need something closer to our situation. Am I correct in assuming that you are a feminist?"

"I am."

"Do you support or oppose the mistreatment of women by men?"

"What do you think? I oppose it."

"Do you oppose it because it is wrong or because you don't like it?"

"I suppose that if I say I oppose it because it is wrong, you will ask me how I can say it is wrong—absolutely wrong."

"That's correct. If you have no absolute standard by which to oppose it, your opposition must spring from your own personal standards, which are not binding on anyone else."

"I will still deny your absolutes. I oppose the mistreatment of women because I don't like it."

Evangelist responded, "You realize this leaves you in a curious position?"

"How do you mean?"

"You are talking with a Christian who believes every-thing the Apostle Paul taught about headship and submis-sion in marriage, but who is also able to say that the mis-treatment of women by men is absolutely wrong. It is wrong in every culture, in every family, and in every age. God will judge it, along with all other sins, at the Last Day. You are a feminist, and yet you are only able to say that you don't like it as a matter of personal preference."

Janice looked at the ground. She seemed distressed.

"There's something else," Evangelist said.

Janice looked up. I could tell she didn't want any more.

"I don't have the time to stand here and play word games! I need to go."

"I don't play with words. I work with them."

Looking at her watch, Janice replied, "Very well. Make your point."

"When there are no absolute standards, it doesn't de-crease the number of conflicts between men. It does, how-ever, change the nature of the conflicts."

"How so?"

"When a conflict arises between those who do not have an absolute standard, the conflict is resolved on the basis of who has the most strength. In other words, might makes right. The loser can *dislike* what has happened, but he can-not consistently *object* to it. This is because his personal pref-erence has no authority over the personal preference of his opponent."

"I don't understand."

"It means that you have adopted a relativistic standard that destroys your ability to make any moral statement about anything. Your objection to the mistreatment of women has been reduced to the same level as your dislike of certain types of food. You don't like chocolate; he does. You don't like rape; he does."

"I don't think the two things compare at all."

"I don't either, but I have a standard by which I can demonstrate that they don't compare. But the person who does not have such a standard is not in the same position."

Evangelist continued, "The Christian position is not that there is some absolute standard in the sky, looking down on us. The message is that these standards come from a personal God. Because we are sinful, we do not measure up to these standards of His. In order to solve the problem caused by our rebellion, God had to send His Son. Jesus Christ died on the cross in order to bring us back to our proper relationship with God the Father."

Janice had been listening quietly, but when Evangelist mentioned God the Father, she started.

"I knew it! All your talk amounts to just one thing. Your view of the universe is that there is some male at the center of things."

Evangelist laughed. "Not at all. God is not male, but he is a Father. Maleness is something that is an aspect of biology. Because the Father is spirit and has no bodily existence, it is improper to say He is male.

"We don't call Him a Father because we named Him after human fathers. It's the other way around. Human fathers derive their name from Him. Even the best human father is just a dim shadow of the authority that constitutes Fatherhood."

This time Janice laughed. "There are no good human fathers. The whole thing is a joke."

Evangelist answered her gently. "It is true that good human fathers are rare. Men have been given a position that they've abused because of their rebellion against God. But if you really object to what they've done, it hardly makes sense to rebel against God along with them."

Janice retorted bitterly, "If this Father does exist, I have no doubt that He is just like his little carbon copies down here—self-centered, arrogant, and proud!"

"You're sounding like an absolutist again. What is wrong with being self-centered, arrogant, and proud?"

"Why do you keep harping on that?"

"Because you want to have it both ways and you cannot. Your bitterness against your earthly father makes you want to strike out against God. So you reject His standards. But when you reject His standards, you discover that you have no basis for objecting to Him. You have to borrow His standards in order to accuse Him. You are like a little child who wants to slap Him in the face, but you have to sit on His lap in order to do so."

Janice was an intelligent woman and had followed Evangelist's argument well. She was obviously torn.

"If I accept what you say, I would have to forgive my father?"

"That's correct. When you have received forgiveness, you must extend it."

"I'm not ready for that." She turned to go.

"May I give you something to think about on the road?"

"I suppose."

"Your father did not give you enough of what you needed. Your Father in the heavens offers to give you all that you need and more. Don't allow the failure of the one to obscure the goodness of the other."

At this, Janice turned and left. I could see the tears in her eyes.

Jack

I turned and saw that Evangelist was being approached by another figure. The person seemed to be quite cheerful and confident.

As the man walked by, he asked Evangelist, "What are you doing out here? It's too nice a day to waste just standing around."

"I'm trying to persuade people to turn around. The road you are on leads to the Abyss," answered Evangelist.

The fellow, whose name was Jack, laughed. "There's no sense in trying to persuade me then. I'm an agnostic."

"Really? What kind of agnostic are you?"

Jack stopped and laughed again. "What do you mean? We don't have a million different denominations like you Christians do."

"I meant that there are three basic types of agnostics. I just wondered which kind you are."

"What are the three types?"

"The first says, 'I don't know, but I wish I did.' The second says, 'I don't know, and I don't care.' The last says, 'I don't know, you don't know, and nobody can know.'"

Jack nodded. "Well, I belong to the last group, but I'd like to hear what you think of the first two."

Evangelist replied, "The first type of agnostic is a searcher. If his searching is honest, he will find the answers he is looking for. No hungry heart ever goes unfed."

"I see. And the second?"

"The second option, I'm afraid, is extremely foolish. This kind of agnostic is too lazy to search for answers. Indeed, he does not even want to be bothered with the questions. To say 'I don't know and don't care' is to admit that you don't even know if not caring is wise."

Jack replied, "Well, we agree on the second option. I object to mindless agnosticism just as I suppose you object to mindless fundamentalism. You *do* object to it, don't you?"

Evangelist smiled at the jibe. "Certainly."

Jack then asked, "So what is your problem with confident agnosticism?"

"Well, it is not exactly *my* problem. It is more like a logical problem."

"What do you mean?"

"You say that man cannot know truth about God, and in the next breath you make a truth claim about God."

"I don't follow you."

"Suppose I said that God is omnipotent, omniscient and omnipresent. What would you say?"

"I would say that you can't know that."

"But your basis for rejecting my truth claim about God is your assumption of another truth claim about God."

"Which is?"

"You are saying that God is such that He cannot be known by man. You are claiming to *know* something about God. This claim to knowledge is inconsistent with your claim to be an agnostic."

Jack started to look a little upset. "Wait a minute! I am saying that *man* cannot know about God. I am making a truth claim about man, not God."

"Then you are in agreement with the Christians."

Jack smiled. "I take it back then." He then grew serious. "What do you mean?"

"I mean that Christians hold that man on his own is incapable of knowledge of God. In order to have truth about God, it must be given to us by God."

"And I say that He has not given it."

"But in order to make the denial, you have to say something true about God. You have to say that God may be there, and if He is, He is the sort of being who is incapable of communicating truth to man. Either that, or He is unwilling to. In either case, you are claiming to know something about God. Where did you get this knowledge about God?"

Jack was silent, so Evangelist continued.

"You say that man is like someone chained to a dungeon wall, incapable of touching the nose of the jailer in front of him. In this, you agree with Christians. But from this you conclude that the jailer is incapable of touching the prisoner's nose. That is not a warranted conclusion. It doesn't follow."

At this Jack retreated. "All right, you made your point. But what do you do with the passages in the Old Testament where God commands various cruelties?"

"I don't do anything with them. I accept them and seek to understand them. But I should point out that your charge of cruelty is not backed up by a careful look at the Old Testament. Besides, to return to the earlier point, how do you *know* that God isn't cruel? I know him, and I know his Word, and I can say that the charge of cruelty is unfounded. You claim to know nothing about him, and then you accuse him. On what basis?"

Jack replied, "I just don't see why God would torture someone forever for refusing to believe something that doesn't make sense to him."

"If that were all there is to it, I would agree with you."

"So why don't you agree?"

"Because it's important to go beyond the surface appearance. *Why* doesn't it make sense? The Christian answer is that mankind *doesn't want it to make sense.* If that is true, then judgment becomes necessary."

"Judgment, eh? Hellfire and brimstone? Quite a religion you've got there."

"You are overlooking something. I'm only *one* of God's

servants who's been stationed on this road to persuade men to turn around. You talk as though God desired nothing more than to populate the Abyss with unfortunate sinners. The reverse is true. When Jesus Christ judges the world, that truth will be completely evident."

"And what truth is that?"

"The One who will judge is the same One who died. That death was for sinners and is offered to sinners. Those sinners who reject it cannot complain of unfairness when God does not apply it to them. You see, they *didn't want it to make sense.*

At this, Jack said goodbye and walked away. He was obviously troubled.

Rev. Howe

Before Jack was even out of sight, I turned and saw another figure approaching Evangelist. He had apparently come up in time to hear the conclusion of the previous conversation.

He carried with him a small book, and wore a clerical collar. Around his neck was a chain with a cross on it, which stood out sharply against his black shirt. He wore a beard and seemed to be a little shy.

As he came up, Evangelist greeted him warmly and he stopped for a moment to visit. Evangelist introduced himself, and the pastor did the same, saying that his name was the Reverend Daniel Howe.

They talked for a moment and Daniel asked what the previous conversation had been about. Evangelist answered that he spent his time on the road trying to persuade travelers to turn around, because the road led to the Abyss. At this, Daniel looked really shocked.

"Are you trying to frighten people? Is that how you minister?"

Evangelist replied that there was nothing wrong with being frightened of the Abyss.

"I am really surprised at you. This is the twentieth century!" Daniel gestured expansively, as though his generation had driven out all superstitions. It was clear he regarded belief in the Abyss as one such superstition, and was much distressed to find it still alive and well.

Evangelist smiled. "I don't understand you. You speak as though the passage of time had the power to dispel truth. But parallel lines did not begin to meet simply because thousands of years have passed since Euclid. Nor does God's Word cease to be true because enough time has passed for men to fall into unbelief."

Daniel replied, somewhat sharply. "It sounds very pious to speak of 'God's Word,' but you neglect the work of very serious biblical scholars. Modern scholarship indicates that those who wrote the Bible were products of their culture. They wrote as fallible men."

"You seem to indicate that you think it is not good to be a product of your culture."

"Why, certainly. If someone writes within the framework of a particular culture, they cannot see it with objectivity."

"And do modern scholars write from within a culture or not?"

Daniel stopped. "What do you mean?"

"You don't trust the apostle Paul because he wrote within the first century. Why don't you mistrust modern scholars for the same reason? They write within the twentieth."

"But modern scholars have good reasons for saying the things they do. They are able to reason objectively."

"So then, you believe it is possible for a writer to transcend the culture he grew up in?"

"Well, yes."

"I'm glad to hear you say that. That is what the biblical writers did." Daniel appeared to be at a loss for words. Evangelist continued. "We know that the biblical writers were willing to challenge their culture with the Word of God, whenever they saw that such a rebuke was needed. They prophesied and spoke against their contemporaries time and again—far more than modern scholars do. If anyone in history was free of contemporay prejudices, they were."

Daniel was shaking his head. "Then you reject modern scholarship?"

Evangelist smiled again. "I certainly do . . . along with

ancient scholarship, and anything else that sets itself up against the knowledge of God."

"What do you mean?"

"Jesus asked a question of the scholars of his day. It was, 'How can you believe if you accept praise from one another, yet make no effort to obtain the praise that comes from the only God?' Scholars love to quote one another, and they fill their books with footnotes from one another's writings. Yet they don't know God."

"But you are advocating ignorance!"

"No, I am opposing ignorance that disguises itself as knowledge. 'Where is the wise man? Where is the scholar? Where is the philosopher of this age? Has not God made foolish the wisdom of the world?' The man who wrote those words was a true scholar—and he knew God."

"So you reject. . . ."

"I reject everything that rebels against God—no matter how many footnotes or big words are contained in the rebellion. God has laid the wisdom of this world into the grave. Modern scholars are vainly trying to bring about a resurrection. It cannot be done."

It was clear that Daniel was indignant, but he was nevertheless shaken. He turned to go. A few paces away, he turned and came back.

"Do you believe that these modern scholars and theologians are Christians?" It was clear that he was braced for an unpleasant answer.

"I will answer you, if you will clarify something for me. Do you believe that Christians exist?"

"Excuse me?"

"I mean, do you believe that there are certain people, uniquely set apart by God, living in the world today?"

"Well, no. I believe that everyone, regardless of their beliefs, has a portion of the divine light within them. Why do you ask?"

"For this reason. I do not want to give unnecessary offense to you. But if you do not really believe that 'Christian' is a genuine category, then you should not take offense if someone excludes you from it, particularly if the person who does so believes that 'Christian' is a term that has great meaning indeed."

"So what are you saying?"

"I cannot speak about all modern scholars because I do not know them. But if they do what you are doing they are not Christians."

Daniel spoke quietly, but it was clear that he was angry. "Because?"

"Because they deny the Lord who died for sinners, and set their face to travel on the road to the Abyss."

"This Lord of yours also said not to judge."

"He said not to judge with a double standard. But a few verses later, he told us to watch for those who will come in sheep's clothing, but who are really ravening wolves. He told us to discern on the basis of fruit."

"Fruit! I have been a pastor in my denomination for 20 years. My father was also a pastor. . . ."

"God can make pastors out of rocks. But in order to make Christians, He sent His Son to die."

Daniel stared at Evangelist for a moment. Evangelist extended his right hand, but Daniel abruptly turned on his heel and left.

Mark

We stood for a while on the solitary road before anyone else appeared. Evangelist seemed to be deep in thought, and from time to time he read from a small black book.

After about a half hour, I spotted a figure in the distance. He appeared to be wearing a white lab coat, and he also was reading something.

He walked up and looked like he was going to go on past without even noticing us. Evangelist approached and offered him a small slip of paper with some writing on it. The man started at being interrupted, and took the paper. He looked at it for a moment, and then handed it back gruffly.

"I'm sorry. I don't have time for fairy tales."

Evangelist smiled. "Neither do I."

"Then don't hand out pieces of paper that talk about God."

"I'm afraid I don't follow you."

"Your tract talks about God. God, by definition, must be a Creator. Creation is a myth and a fairy tale. Your piece of paper must therefore be a fairy tale. Fair enough?"

The man turned to go, but stopped abruptly at Evangelist's comment. "If you object to 'fairy tales,' then why do you borrow from them?"

The man whirled in his tracks. "I borrow from nothing. My philosophy is built on reason, not some . . . some book!"

"But that is my point exactly."

"What!"

"Your earlier chain of reasoning, and your statement just now, indicate that you believe in the validity of reason."

"That is correct."

"Why is that?"

"What do you mean, 'Why is that?'"

"Do you believe in the theory of evolution?"

"I certainly do. Science has settled the matter beyond question."

"So you believe that all we see around us is the result of time and chance acting on matter?"

"I do."

"And that nothing exists unless it is the result of this process?"

"Correct."

"So this is what lies behind my earlier question. Why do you believe in the validity of reason? How can time and chance, acting on matter, produce reason?"

The man stopped and thought for a moment. It was clear that he thought Evangelist was just playing with words, and that the trick would become apparent in a few minutes. Evangelist continued. "If you see a chemical reaction in the laboratory, it does not occur to you to say that the reaction is either true or false. It just is. According to you, my Christian beliefs are just a complex chemical reaction within my head. So why do you think them to be false? And your beliefs are simply a different chemical reaction. So why do you think they are true?"

The man was clearly intrigued. He introduced himself (his name was Mark), walked over to a rock at the side of the road, and sat down. He then asked, "Is this then what you mean when you say I am borrowing reason?"

"That is correct. It is not my purpose now to argue the theory of evolution. We can do that another time. My question is why the proponents of evolution borrow reason from theism to argue their case."

Mark was clearly an intelligent man, but this was a type

of reasoning that was entirely novel. Nevertheless, he took the argument to the next step. "So then, you do not seek to defend your God, or the doctrine of Creation, with your reason."

Evangelist smiled. "You understand well. I believe in God so that I may retain my reason. He does not depend on reason. Reason depends on Him. Reason flows out of His nature." He continued. "For those who do not believe in God the only consistent position is nihilism. Of course, if there is no God there is nothing wrong with being inconsistent. If all standards have collapsed, it hardly makes sense to keep the standard of consistency. After reason has departed, anything goes."

Mark sat there chuckling for a few moments. "You are right . . . anything goes. And that includes rejecting your God, which I continue to do, even though I am in your debt for the argument. Thank you." At this Mark got up to go.

Evangelist stopped him with a motion of his hand. "You are neglecting something else."

"And that is?"

"Before, you had a reason for rejecting God—or at least you thought you did. Now you may continue to rebel, but you have been stripped of your weapons. The only thing standing between you and God is your unwillingness to have anything to do with Him."

"You misunderstand me. I only reject Him because He does not exist. My 'unwillingness' has nothing to do with it."

"And what are your reasons for this belief that He does not exist?"

Mark rubbed his chin. "I see your point."

"Your atheism must rest on an unsupported presupposition, not on any claim to reason. In order to build it on the foundation of reason you have to borrow from theism. But if you base it on this unsupported presupposition, then you have to admit that you have no reason to speak of God's existence, one way or another. And yet, in spite of this lack, you defy Him anyway. Whence the defiance?"

"But when you ask me to defend this attitude, you are asking for reasons."

"Correct."

"Why? According to you, those who hold this position are under no obligation to give reasons."

"I ask for their reasons because I want them to know their position. I want people to say out loud that they have no reason to defy God, and that yet they defy Him anyway. Call it spiritual reality therapy."

"And what do you do with those who are willing to say it?"

"I commend them. And give them something else to think about on the road."

Mark laughed out loud. "I wish there were more Christians like you. What do you want me to think about?"

"I want you to ponder your sins."

"Excuse me?"

"If you have no reasons for rebellion against God, then the source of that rebellion must be elsewhere. I suggest that you investigate the area of morality. Perhaps you don't wish to live the way God insists we live?"

Mark turned away, shaking his head. About ten yards away, he turned back for a parting comment. "You are presupposing that God exists."

"Certainly."

Robert

I was tired, so I found a comfortable, shaded place under a nearby tree and took a short nap. When I awoke, I discovered that Evangelist was in a conversation with four boisterous young men. The conversation had apparently been going for a while, but it was not hard to pick up on the character of the exchange.

"What about the people in Africa who have never heard of your God? What happens to them?" The speaker was a large fellow, and slightly overweight. His companions hooted at the point they thought he had scored.

Evangelist replied, "People do not receive condemnation *because they haven't heard*. They are condemned already."

Evangelist's adversary pointed a finger. "And what is that supposed to mean?"

"It means that hearing the message is the solution to the problem. The problem is sin. Not everyone has heard the Christian message. But everyone sins."

"Do you mean to say that *everyone* is condemned?"

"Yes. And those who die without Christ are people who do not know of the solution to their problem. But they are very aware of the problem—sin is to the human race what water is to a fish."

At this statement, the young men began to gesture in an agitated manner. All of them began talking at once until their leader (whose name was Robert) managed to drown

49

them out. "How is this supposed to solve the problem? Aren't they still condemned?"

"Yes, but they are not condemned for what they did not know. They are condemned for their failure to live up to what they did know. And the only solution for that state of condemnation is the death and resurrection of Jesus Christ.

"Look at it this way. Suppose for a moment that you had developed a cure for cancer. You took it into a cancer ward and you gave it away to half the patients. What would happen to the patients who did not receive the gift?"

"I suppose they would die. Is that your answer?"

"That is exactly right. Now, what would they die of?"

"They would die of cancer."

"That is also correct. They would not die of 'not taking medicine.' Their refusal to take the medicine affects whether they die, but it is not the cause of death. It is the disease which kills, and in the case of the human race, the disease is sin."

One of the other young men apparently decided it was time to change the subject. "That's just your interpretation. Anyone can read the Bible and get whatever interpretation he wants from it. This just happens to be yours."

Evangelist smiled. "What do you mean?"

"I mean that when someone hauls out a Bible we can't be sure that what they say is true. There are too many interpretations to be sure which one is right."

Evangelist answered him, "Suppose we had a room with one hundred copies of this translation of the Bible." Evangelist held up his worn little black book. "Suppose further that we put one hundred people from various backgrounds into the room with the Bibles. Now how many different interpretations will we get of what they read?"

"I think we will get one hundred different interpretations."

"Well perhaps it wouldn't be quite so bad, but let's grant it for the sake of the argument. Now here is the question. Where is the variable? Is it in the Bibles or is it in the men?"

"Well, it is in the men."

"So then we should say that men are not to be trusted because they come up with so many interpretations?"

"No. . . ." The speaker looked trapped and glanced at his companions for help. It was not forthcoming.

Evangelist continued. "It puzzles me that those who object most strongly to all the 'different interpretations' continue to trust those who are the source of the problem. They trust in men, not in God. The problem you mention is a real problem, but the solution is to stay as close to the Bible's teaching as you can."

The four young men were not as boisterous as they were before, but they did seem a little more hostile. Robert abruptly changed the subject. "Where did Cain get his wife?"

Evangelist laughed. "Do you really want to know?"

"Yes, I do."

"He married his sister."

"But isn't that incest?"

"It is prohibited by God's law now. At the time of Cain it was not prohibited—and for good reason."

This line of argument did not get to the conclusion, apparently because Robert decided that there was no sense in it. Evangelist seemed to know what he was talking about.

"Well, what about the problem of suffering? How can a loving God let innocent people suffer? Right now there are people that are starving to death in Africa. What about it?"

"It's strange that you should mention that." Evangelist smiled. "Our gathering of believers is working on a collection that will help with famine relief in Africa. If you joined us that effort would certainly be helped." He looked at each of the four men, and each shook his head. Evangelist continued. "Consider your argument closely then. You seem to be saying that man is basically good even though he rebels against God's law. You also want to believe that God has a moral problem because He doesn't wave a magic wand and remove the consequences of man's ongoing disobedience. You think that man is basically good even though he is the direct cause of these sorts of problems. But God, who merely allows man to eat his own cooking, is therefore accused of great injustice."

"But He could just speak the word (if He exists) and all these problems would disappear."

"The *consequences* of sin would disappear. But in order to deal with *sin itself*, He sent His Son to die on the cross. He did this to change men, but some men will have none of it. Some don't want to be changed."

The four looked at each other, and decided it was time to go. They told Evangelist that they had to go drinking and couldn't afford to waste any more time with him.

Evangelist smiled. "Well, I'll pray for you."

Three of the young men were already down the road, but Robert heard the last comment. He whirled around. "Don't do that!"

"Does it matter to you whether I pray? I thought you didn't believe I was getting through."

A strange look came over Robert's face. He then turned and ran after his companions.

Jim and Sarah

Evangelist turned and sat down on a rock beside the road. He seemed to be waiting and resting until the next conversation. From where I stood I could see a couple heading toward us. They seemed to be arguing, and not too quietly either.

Evangelist stood up as they came closer and approached them. They were so involved in their quarrel they didn't see him until he spoke to them.

"Good afternoon," Evangelist said. "May I help you?"

The man looked up, startled. "Well, yes! You could start by minding your own business."

Evangelist smiled. "I beg your pardon. There was no indication that you desired your conversation to be kept secret."

At this the woman blushed and apologized. "I'm sorry. We didn't mean to broadcast our difficulties. You can't help us. I don't think anyone can help us."

"I don't know if that is true. What are your names?"

The woman responded, "My name is Sarah. This is my future ex-husband, Jim. Who are you?"

"My name is Evangelist. I travel on the road, waiting to help people in situations like yours."

Sarah glanced at her husband, who was still scowling, and asked if he wanted to talk with Evangelist. He didn't look too happy about it, but agreed.

Evangelist began by asking how long they had been married, and how long they had been unhappy together. They responded that they had been married about three years, and both agreed that about six months into the marriage things had started to go downhill. Evangelist asked them what they argued about and learned that they argued about everything.

Evangelist then asked them if they wanted good advice or good news.

At this Jim looked up, appearing interested. "What do you mean?"

"I mean that there are two approaches to take in helping couples with troubled marriages. One is to tell them what they're doing wrong. The unhappy couple is told, 'Do this, don't do that.' This is the good advice approach. The other is to tell them of someone who can help them by giving them the power to do what is right. This is the good news approach."

Evangelist looked at Sarah. "Have you read any books on how to have a happy marriage?"

Sarah laughed. "I have read so many books I can't remember them all. There have been books on finances, sex, communication, intimacy, and openness." She glared at Jim. "He hasn't read any of them."

Evangelist ignored her last comment and asked if any of the books had helped.

"Well, I learned a lot."

"But that's not what I asked. Have they helped? Are you happier or not?"

"What do you mean?"

"Have you learned things in the books that were good, but that you didn't have the power to put into practice?"

"Yes, that happens a lot."

"So you have received much good advice, and no good news?"

"Yes."

Here Evangelist turned to Jim and asked what he thought of the books.

Jim said he avoided them for two reasons. "They tell me what I need to do, and I already know more than I am able to do. If I can't choke down what I already have on my plate, why should I fill it up with more?"

Evangelist asked for his second reason.

"Well, one of the things we fight about a lot is the fact that Sarah wants me to be more of a leader—to show more initiative. Then she gives me all this stuff to read. She wants me to be a leader—as long as she gets to lead me into it."

At this Sarah started to sputter, but Evangelist motioned to her, and she became quiet.

"Did you understand the distinction I made between good advice and good news?"

Jim answered, "Yes. But there is a problem with what you say. Anything you tell us would have to go into the good advice category. We are the only two people in this marriage, and if it is going to be done, we will have to do it. And we don't seem to have the ability."

Jim then turned to go, but stopped when Evangelist asked, "What would you say if I told you that the problem with your marriage is that there are only two people in it?"

Sarah began to look upset. "You're not talking about open marriage, are you? Seeing someone else?"

Evangelist laughed. "Yes, but not the way you think. I am talking about God. If God were in your lives, you would have the power to do what He requires of you."

"How can that make any difference? We have religious friends who are every bit as unhappy as we are."

"I wasn't referring to a religion empty of a relationship with God. Most religious people use their religion as a source of good advice, and the good advice only condemns them when they fail. This mistake is even made by professing Christians, who should know better."

"So how is your message any different? Are you saying that the good advice is bad?"

"Not at all." Evangelist turned and pointed to an apple tree beside the road. "Do you see this tree? Does it produce apples or not?"

Jim laughed. "Of course it does."

"Does it produce apples because it is an apple tree, or does it try to produce apples in an attempt to become an apple tree?"

"The apples are a result of what the tree is."

Evangelist then pointed to a small bush beside the road. "Can this bush become an apple tree by producing apples?"

"Of course not."

"Suppose it tried to. What would you say to it?"

Sarah interrupted. "I suppose you have a point in all this?"

Evangelist nodded. "What would you say?"

"I would say the attempt was futile."

"Would this mean that you disliked apples?"

"Certainly not. It only means that I know that apples are not grown on bushes."

"Just so. In the same way, the good advice you have received is truly good. But you do not have the power to put it into practice. You are a bush trying to produce apples."

"What can be done about it?"

"There is someone who has the authority and power to change you. He does so when you come to Him on the basis of the death and resurrection of His Son."

Both Jim and Sarah seemed to be following the argument, so Evangelist went on.

"Marriage does not change what you are. It does, however, amplify what you are. This is why so many have trouble in marriage. When they come into an intimate relationship with another person, their self-centeredness is amplified many times over. *No amount of marriage counseling can change that.*

"A marriage can only be transformed when the individuals in that marriage are transformed. You cannot have your marriage transformed until each of you as individuals come to God through Christ. Then, as a result, the marriage will be changed. The good news must come first, and then the good advice. Until then, the only value that good advice has is that it reveals to you how far short of God's requirements you fall."

Jim and Sarah stepped back for a moment and talked quietly. Then they turned and thanked Evangelist. Jim said, "There is much in what you say. We need some time to think it over, but we will be back." At this, they went on. As they left, their conversation was subdued. It was clear that this approach to marriage was not going to have the same effect as the other things they had tried. This time, things would be different.

Dorothy

Evangelist seemed a little tired, and he sat down for a few moments by the side of the road. But he had not been there long when another figure appeared in the distance. As she got closer, Evangelist rose to greet her. She was a middle-aged woman, fairly stout, but with a look of a ready and quick intelligence about her face.

She stopped and took a brief look at the paper which Evangelist had handed her, laughed, and returned it. "I know some other people who could use this more than I!"

Evangelist looked at her questioningly.

"Why don't you hand these things out at churches? There is no shortage of sinners there!" At this, the woman, whose name was Dorothy, turned to go.

Evangelist stopped her with a question. "What kind of sinners are you talking about?"

Dorothy smiled. "Doesn't matter. Any sin will do when you are making a hypocrite. Why should I want to become a Christian? Look at all the hypocrites!"

Evangelist nodded soberly. "You are quite right. There are many. But your argument is lost on me. What do hypocrites have to do with it?"

Dorothy was clearly interested in his question. She stopped, and folded her arms. "Hypocrites have everything to do with it. They proclaim themselves to be good Christians, and then live like the devil. Why should I want to join them?"

"Well, you shouldn't, but then again, no one is asking you to."

She shook her head.

Evangelist went on. "Do you have any money on you?"

"Well, yes."

"Why do you do that? You are apparently arguing, with regard to Christianity, that the mere existence of a counterfeit is grounds for rejecting the genuine. Surely you are aware that many counterfeit dollar bills exist. So why do you still seek to retain the genuine dollar bills?"

"I can't help that. Everyone needs money."

"True enough. And everyone needs God."

"But you are assuming that He exists. I know that genuine money exists, and that I need it. I don't know that there are any genuine Christians."

"You are quite right when you say that I assume that He exists. Everyone does that, even those who deny Him. But have you ever thought that the mere existence of hypocrites is an evidence that there are genuine Christians?"

"How so?"

"Well, counterfeiters don't spend their time forging brown shopping bags. They are not valuable enough. But they do spend their time on paper currency. Why? Because there is a real currency valuable enough to counterfeit. In the same way, hypocrites testify that genuine Christianity exists, and that it is a valuable thing. This is no proof, but it is evidence. If you want to base your actions on the behavior of hypocrites, it is at least worth considering."

Dorothy shook her head again. "I don't know. I don't think I could take being on the same team with all those fakers."

"Well, that's another thing. Whose team are you on now?"

"What do you mean?"

"Well, suppose for a moment that God is there, and that

He did reveal His Word to us in the Bible."

"That's a big suppose, but okay."

"That means there are two ways of living. We can either live the way God says to, or we can refuse. There are two teams—one in submission to God and the other not."

"Fair enough."

"Now, what does God think of hypocrisy? Is He for it, or against it?"

"Well, against it, I suppose."

"Correct. So hypocrites are on the other team?"

"That's right."

"So what team are those on who reject God because of all the hypocrites? Whose team have they refused to join?"

"God's."

"Now because there are only two teams, this means that the hypocrites are on the same team with those who have refused to have anything to do with God because of hypocrisy. Is that fair?"

"I guess so." Dorothy was looking uncomfortable.

"Now you said earlier that you couldn't handle being on the same team with all those fakers. But it looks now as though you already are."

Dorothy didn't say anything.

Evangelist pressed the point home. "That's one of the reasons why I couldn't handle becoming a non-Christian— all the hypocrites in church." He grinned.

Dorothy smiled back, a little grimly. "You sound like you believe that hypocrisy is no problem at all for the Christian church."

"Not at all. It is a major problem. But it is a *practical* problem, not a theological one. If there are weeds in my garden, I have a problem. But it does not lead me to question the existence of lettuce." Dorothy laughed, and Evangelist went on. "There is another point worth considering. Have you ever noticed that Christians are in a no-win situation here, at least in the minds of those non-Christians observing?"

"What do you mean?"

"What would happen if the pastor of some Christian church started living with the church organist, and nothing really was done about it? What would the non-Christian say about it?"

"I suppose he would accuse them all of hypocrisy."

"That is quite right, and he would be correct in the accusation. But what would happen if the church disciplined them—defrocking the minister, and excommunicating them both? What would be said now?"

Dorothy shook her head. "I am not sure what you're getting at."

"Why, the church would be accused of being a bunch of self-righteous fundamentalists. Who do they think they are? Is such an accusation possible?"

Dorothy nodded. "Yes, that could happen."

"In other words, if Christians take action against some rank hypocrisy they run the risk of being labelled judgmental. If they do not, then they join the ranks of the hypocrites themselves. It is a good thing that Christians are to follow the teaching of Scripture. If we were required to obey the world on this matter, it would be hard to know what to do." Evangelist continued. "There is also one other difficulty. Sharp discipline is required by the Bible for cases of moral rebellion. But there are many people within the church with many problems which are less overt. Such people must be helped, but the help must come through other means—encouragement, admonishment, and so forth. In the meantime, such struggling individuals can be uncharitably labelled by outsiders as hypocrites. It has been well said that the church is a hospital for sinners, not a rest home for saints. To reject Christ because the church has sin of this sort in it is like rejecting hospitals because they are full of sick people."

At this, Dorothy smiled and turned away. "You have given me much to think about on the road. Thank you for your time."

Once again, Evangelist offered her the paper he had given her at first. This time she took it.

Bill

After a short time, another man approached us. He walked up to us, and when Evangelist offered him a small pamphlet he took it and looked at it. He then took one out of his pocket and gave to Evangelist. They both took a minute to look over what the other had given.

The other man, whose name was Bill, broke the silence. "Do you realize that legalism never got anyone into heaven?"

Evangelist smiled. "I certainly do. But why do you make the point?"

"Well, because you say here that someone becomes a Christian when they submit to the lordship of Jesus Christ. And that is legalism."

"Before I answer, how do you say someone becomes a Christian?"

"The answer is the simple message of grace. If anyone honestly prays and asks Jesus to save them, He will, regardless of good works before *or after* the prayer."

"What does Jesus save them from?"

"He saves them from the penalty of sin. He saves them from Hell."

"You are saying that He saves them from the penalty of sin, but not from the power of sin?"

"That is correct. Deliverance from the power of sin comes *if* the Christian makes Jesus the Lord of His life. But if he doesn't, Jesus is still his Savior."

"Regardless of whether his life is changed at all?"

"That is correct. *Salvation is not by works.*"

"True enough. You are referring to. . . ."

"Ephesians. 'For it is by grace you have been saved, through faith—and this not from yourselves, it is the gift of God—not by works, so that no one can boast.'"

"I quite agree. And what does the next verse say?"

"Excuse me?"

"What does the next verse say?"

"I . . . I'm not sure."

"'For we are God's workmanship, created in Christ Jesus to do good works, which God prepared in advance for us to do.' The Bible is quite clear that we are not saved *by* good works. But it is equally clear that we are saved *to* good works. And if the good works are absent, so is salvation."

"But don't you see that you are basing salvation on good works?"

"Not at all. It is the other way around. Good works are based on salvation."

Bill seemed exasperated. "Let's look at it from another angle. You are saying that if Jesus is not Lord of someone's life then He is not that person's Savior."

"Correct. Christ cannot be received on the installment plan."

"And you are claiming to be a Christian?"

"That is also correct."

"Now answer me honestly here. Have you sinned since you became a Christian—since Christ became 'Lord of your life?'"

"I certainly have, I'm ashamed to say."

"Well, how can you say that Christ was the Lord of your life at those times?"

"By saying that Christ's lordship in my life is not dependent on my behavior. My behavior is dependent on His lordship."

"What?"

"Let me illustrate. I have a small boy—he is around seven

years old. Has he ever disobeyed me?"

"Well, of course."

"When he does, does he cease to be my son?"

"No."

"Do I cease to exercise my 'lordship' as a father over him?"

"Well, no again. I suppose you discipline him."

"Correct. When he is obedient, he acknowledges my 'lordship.' And when he is disobedient he experiences my 'lordship' through discipline. But there is no escape for him from my authority."

"So you are saying that Christ's lordship has nothing to do with whether we sin."

"Not quite. True, the debate is not over whether Christians can sin. Rather, the debate is over whether a Christian can sin without being disciplined by his Father. When someone becomes a Christian, the Holy Spirit makes that person into a new creation, and loving discipline begins. For true Christians the discipline begins immediately, meaning of course that there is an immediate change in lifestyle."

"And if there is no change, no evidence of discipline. . . ."

"There is no salvation. No holiness, no heaven. Lack of holiness is evidence that the Holy Spirit is not present. For when He is present He leads us in putting to death the misdeeds of the body."

"But surely you agree that there are many Christians who agree with what I am saying."

"That is correct. They agree with what you say, but they are not traveling in the same direction you are."

"What do you mean by that?"

"Christianity is full of teachers who are much better than their theology. They agree with you verbally, but *their lives do not reflect it*. They do not live the way they teach. Still, Jesus said that men like that should be considered least in the kingdom of heaven. I feel part of the reason is that those who listen to them are not always so fortunate as they are."

"Well, how do you make the distinction?"

"By the direction they travel. If they are traveling to the City, I count them my brother, regardless of destructive theology. But if they are traveling toward the Abyss, it is a different story." Here Evangelist pointed down the road in the direction Bill had been traveling. The point was not lost on him.

"So you are saying that I am not a Christian?" Bill looked both angry and upset.

"Jesus said that we were to judge on the basis of fruit. That fruit does not include decisions, professions, prayers, walking the aisle, and so forth. To rely on such things— things men can do on their own—is to base salvation on works. Extremely paltry works, I might add."

"You say there must be fruit. What do you call fruit?"

"Love, righteousness, joy, kindness. . . ."

"So you are saying that in order to be saved, a person must work at cultivating these virtues?"

"No, I am saying that when God saves a person He *always* begins to produce such fruit in that person's life. The Christian works out his salvation because *God is at work in him*."

"You are putting people back under the law! And the Bible says we are not under law, but under grace."

"But again, what does that passage say in the same breath?"

Bill was glowering now. "I don't know. What does it say?"

"It says that sin shall not be your master. Why? Because we are not under law, but under grace. Your position represents grace as giving freedom to sin—allowing sin to be lord, which it must be if Jesus is not Lord. The Bible represents grace as giving freedom *from* sin."

"You are saying that grace is not a free gift at all!"

"Not at all. The question is not whether grace is a gift. The question concerns how big the gift is. I am saying that the gift is immense—and it includes the righteousness of God's people."

Bill turned to go. He was very unhappy. Evangelist

stopped him with a last comment.

"Consider what you want. You want to arrive at last at the City but you don't want to walk in that direction. How can that be?"

Bill turned away again. It was clear that he was not at all sure.

Miriam

When I looked up again I found that Evangelist was deep in conversation with someone else. She was a young woman, and she looked very earnest. She was somewhat attractive. She was holding something in the palm of her hand, and holding it out for Evangelist to see. It was clear she was a true believer in something.

"And what is that?" he asked.

"A crystal." She was patient.

"And does it have spiritual significance?"

"It certainly does. Of course everything has spiritual significance, but some things—like this—have extraordinary power."

Evangelist nodded, but his interest was not the crystal. "What is your name?"

"My name is Miriam."

"Well, Miriam, you say that everything has spiritual significance. Why is that?"

"Because everything is One. The universe is God and God is the universe."

"So you are a pantheist?"

Miriam laughed. "You Christians are so obsessed with labels! But if it helps you understand . . . yes, I am a pantheist."

"So then you believe that everything is as important as everything else?"

"That is correct. There is no such thing as insignificance. Everything—everyone—is part of the One. Some deny this, and others believe it. But the enlightened are those who *see* it."

Evangelist nodded again. "So that is why you single out some objects—like crystals—for special attention. They help you on the path toward this enlightenment."

Miriam agreed, so Evangelist went on. "When you say that everything is part of the One, do you mean *everything?*"

"Yes, I do. There are no exceptions. You seem to have trouble with that?"

"Well, yes. There is a problem in the area of morality."

"What are you talking about?"

"The belief that everything is One is not consistent with a belief in morality."

Miriam was indignant. "How can you say that?"

"Everything is One?"

"Yes."

"So the apparent diversity we see around us is just *maya*—illusion?"

"Yes, that's true too."

"If everything is One, then all the various manifestations of plurality should be rejected as illusory? This and that, mine and yours, here and there?"

"True, but what does that have to do with morality?"

"When a man pours a cup of coffee, is he acting as part of the One?"

"Yes."

"And when a man rapes and murders a woman, is he acting as part of the One?"

Miriam stopped. She didn't want to answer.

Evangelist repeated the question. "Do you believe that this too is part of the One?"

"Well, yes."

"And that one mark of an enlightened individual would be the ability to see this, not as an 'evil' action, but as an equal part of the ultimate One?"

"Yes." Miriam was looking around.

"So if acknowledgment of the One leads to the abolition of all distinctions, it must also include the abolition of the distinction between good and evil."

Miriam looked troubled, but she replied gamely. "It is not just the distinction that is abolished, both good and evil themselves are abolished. That is, the enlightened person comes to understand that they are *both* part of the One."

"So on this side of enlightenment, what difference does it make how we behave? It is all the same."

"A person who rapes and murders does so because he is caught up in the illusion. If he refrained, he could pursue enlightenment."

"But that raises two more questions. Why could he not pursue enlightenment through rape and murder? Followers of Zen meditate on a koan—'What is the sound of one hand clapping?'—in order to break out of rational categories. Why could not someone do the same here—a sort of criminal koan?" Miriam was looking miserable, but Evangelist continued. "The second question is this: Suppose he doesn't choose to pursue enlightenment. Isn't this lack of pursuit also part of the One? Why be enlightened?"

"What do you mean, 'Why be enlightened?'"

"Words like 'ought' and 'ought not' are part of the illusion. But to get away from the illusion, people say things like 'We ought to be enlightened,' indicating that they are still caught in the trap. The only consistent way out of the trap is to recognize that *nothing matters*. But if *that's* true, then it doesn't matter if we get out of the trap."

"I think you must enjoy playing your little word games!"

"I don't mean to upset you."

"Then why all these questions?"

"Because you obviously believe that everything is One, and that others should join you in this belief. But before others join you, I am suggesting they should ask a few questions."

"But the questions you ask show that you are trapped by

Western rationalism—you are playing with logic."

"It is true that I am using logic. But your answers show that you are trapped by this same 'Western rationalism.' The only difference is that you are uncomfortable with it, and use it inconsistently."

"I don't know what you mean."

"If a man says, 'This, not that,' he is accused of putting everything into rational categories. But if someone with your position says the statement is not true, he also is saying 'This, not that.' All men make distinctions because they must. When someone denies distinctions, he is making a distinction. There is no escape from the way God made the world."

Miriam looked at Evangelist with exasperation, turned on her heel, and left.

Paul

For some time no one passed by, and Evangelist began to walk slowly uphill in the direction of the City. He sang softly as he walked. After about two hours, he saw someone coming toward him and slowed down to greet him.

The man he spoke to was young and seemed to be a studious sort. Evangelist asked what his occupation was, and Paul (for that was his name) replied that he was a graduate student in paleontology.

Evangelist asked him if he was at all interested in spiritual things, and Paul shook his head.

"I used to be—before I went to graduate school. But now I've learned so much that it makes my earlier faith seem, well . . . childish. Sunday School is one thing, science is another."

"What sort of things have you learned which conflict with biblical faith?"

"Well, the Bible says that God created everything in six days, and yet the world abounds with fossil evidence to the contrary."

"How does the fossil evidence conflict with the biblical account?"

"It shows the emergence of complex life forms over eons. The Bible doesn't say it happened that way. I know some of you Christians try to harmonize what the Bible says and what evolutionary science says, but I've looked again and again, and I just can't get them to fit together."

"I quite agree—they don't fit. Even if you accept that each day in Genesis is an age, the order is still all wrong. For example, in Genesis life doesn't begin in the sea."

"I'm glad to hear you say that. So how can you still believe the biblical account?"

"You said the fossil record shows the emergence of complex life forms over eons, correct?"

"That is right."

"There are two problems with your statement. The first is in your phrase 'the fossil record shows' and the second with the word 'eons.'"

Paul looked pleased at the unexpected appearance of an intelligent adversary. "What do you mean?"

"The fossil record *shows* nothing. Evolutionary scientists have made an assumption, and seek to understand the fossil record in the light of that assumption. Suppose you were on a dig two thousand years from now, and you discovered, in different strata, a Shetland pony, a quarterhorse, a thoroughbred, and a Clydesdale. What would you be tempted to think?"

"Well, to be honest, the temptation would be to arrange them in some sort of evolutionary way—as though the big horse evolved from the smaller one."

"And given the assumption of evolution, such an arrangment would come easily. Now has the fossil record *shown* you this arrangment, or is it merely consistent with it?"

"It is merely consistent."

"Correct. After all, the fossils *could* be related. But the fossils themselves do not teach us the relation, if it exists. *That* is determined by our assumptions."

"Fair enough. But the evolutionary assumption is the best assumption to make—I mean it gives the best explanation of the data."

"Perhaps. I'll grant it for the sake of the argument. But the assumption should be admitted. The evolutionist *begins* with an evolutionary assumption, which causes him to see the evidence in a certain way. He does not look at the evidence 'objectively' and come to an evolutionary conclusion. This means that those with a different assumption should not be ignored, or dismissed as flat-earthers."

Paul smiled. "What if they are flat-earthers?"

"Then that should be proven by meeting their objections head on."

"All right. How can a different assumption better explain the fossil record?"

"In the ordinary course of events, do animals usually fossilize when they die?"

"No, usually there is some sort of unusual event—like a volcanic eruption, or a flood."

"So localized fossilization is much more likely to occur in some sort of local cataclysm than in ordinary circumstances?"

"That is correct."

"So if we find widespread fossilization it would be reasonable to infer a widespread cataclysm?"

"Well. . . ." Paul suddenly caught a glimpse of where Evangelist was going.

"And if we find fossil graveyards with millions of animals jammed together, it would be reasonable to infer a cataclysm of titanic proportions?"

"So you really believe that story about Noah and the ark? You really are trapped in Sunday School!"

"Well, it happens that I do believe the story, but my concern here is with the fossil evidence, not the Bible story."

"What do you mean, 'The fossil evidence'?"

"We need to understand the nature of such evidence. Is the evidence supportive, or conclusive? I believe it to be supportive, and the assumption it supports best happens to be the biblical account of creation, followed by a global flood. So the fossil evidence doesn't *prove* there was a global flood, but it certainly is consistent with that idea."

"You said you had another problem with my initial comment—something about 'eons.'"

"Yes. Evolutionists make another major assumption as well. This assumption has to do with how fossils are dated. The process is represented as 'objective science,' but the whole thing is built on an unproven assumption."

"And what is that?"

"Suppose we saw a man walk by us here on the road. Do we know his present location?"

"Certainly."

"And can we clock his rate of speed?"

"Of course."

"On the basis of this information, can we say how long he has been on the road?"

"Well, no. For that we need to know where he started."

"So in order to calculate how long this man has been on the road, we need more information than his current location and speed."

"That's right."

"And in order to date how old a rock is we would also need more than current location and speed?"

"Wait a minute. Rocks are a different matter. What do you mean by current location and speed?"

"When a scientist dates a rock he does so by measuring the present ratio of parent element to daughter element (current location), and by knowing the half life of the radioactive parent element (speed). These are the only two things that can be scientifically ascertained. But in order to date the rock, he must know where the rock started (that is, what the initial ratio between the parent and daughter elements was). And that cannot be known scientifically—it must be *assumed*."

"So you are denying the accuracy of radiometric dating?"

"That is exactly what I am doing."

"You keep referring to 'assumptions.' Why is that?"

"Because that is where all thinking starts. The facts do not lead us to our various assumptions; our various assumptions affect how we view the 'facts.' It doesn't matter what these assumptions are called—presuppositions, premises, whatever—the result is the same."

"So the facts don't matter?"

"I didn't say that. If the starting assumption is the true one, then the facts will fit perfectly. If the assumption is false, then they will not. If they do not, then that should cause the investigator to reexamine his starting assumption. Evidence is important—but it is not the starting point. It cannot be approached 'objectively.'"

"I see. And what are the basic assumptions which conflict in the creation/evolution debate?"

"It is very simple really. The choice is between an infinite, personal Father, and infinite, chaotic matter."

Paul thanked Evangelist, and shaking his head, he walked slowly down the road. He looked thoughtful.

Michael

When he looked up, Evangelist found himself gazing at a young man walking on the other side of the road. When the man saw Evangelist, he apparently understood what he was doing. He immediately crossed the road and asked for one of the papers that Evangelist had. Evangelist handed one over gladly.

The young man looked it over carefully. When he was done, he asked, "What church do you represent?"

Evangelist replied, "I represent no church."

"You don't belong to a church?"

"I didn't say that. I said I did not *represent* a church. I seek to be found in Jesus Christ, and consequently to represent Him. All others who do the same belong to His church, and are members of one another."

"I see. So what do you think of the Catholic church?"

Evangelist smiled. "I take it that you're a Catholic."

The young man, whose name was Michael, smiled back. "That is correct. Do you have an opinion on it?"

Evangelist nodded. "I certainly do. But I also have no desire to give unnecessary offense. Do you mind discussing such things?"

Michael laughed confidently. "Not at all. The Catholic church has withstood sectarian teaching for thousands of years. Proceed."

Evangelist began, "Perhaps we should begin with agreement. Catholicism should not necessarily be evaluated on the basis of the immorality of any of its professors—from the Renaissance popes to college students who get drunk Saturday night and go to confession the next morning. Are we agreed?"

Michael nodded. "I am glad to hear you say that. Every religion has its hypocrites."

Evangelist continued. "Such behavior can only be an issue if it can be shown that there is a connection between such behavior and the official teachings of the church. But *that* cannot be known at the beginning of the discussion."

"Fair enough."

"It is also important to distinguish between a movement of renewal and a movement of reformation. A devout Catholic could easily object to rampant immorality, and seek to correct the abuses by calling Catholics back to a stricter standard. In none of this would he be violating any standard of the church." Michael nodded again, and Evangelist continued. "Many monastic orders began out of such a concern for renewal. Fierce denunciations of immorality in the Catholic church are not a practice limited to opponents of the church. Such monastic orders have repeatedly sought to call Catholics back to a renewal of their devotion."

"Do you believe there are any such "renewal" movements today?"

"I certainly do. It is not monastic, but the charismatic movement within the church is a fine example."

"I couldn't agree more. I am part of that movement. We do seek a renewal of spiritual life within the church. But what objection could you possibly have to this?"

"Remember that I distinguished between renewal and reformation?"

"Yes."

"And that renewal addresses problems of lifestyle? Immorality, flagging devotion, and so forth?"

"Yes again. So what does reformation, as you call it, address?"

"Reformation addresses the *teaching* of the church. The lifestyle abuses are only considered as the fruit of the false teaching."

"What would you consider as examples of 'reformation'?"

"Well, Francis of Assisi was concerned with renewal. The Waldensians, Huss, Wycliffe, Luther, and Calvin were concerned with reformation."

"But the men you name were schismatics. It is true that there were moral abuses which troubled them, but they still left the true church."

"Not quite. The abuses were not the central issue. Remember, they could have addressed those abuses only, and earned a place of honor in Catholic history. They could have been heroes of renewal. *The real issue was justification by faith alone.* Just as the Jews ceased to be true Jews with the crucifixion of their own Christ, so the Catholics ceased to be Catholic when they refused to acknowledge the gospel of Christ. Of course, for both groups the way of repentance is open."

"You *say* they rejected the gospel. But by what authority do you define the gospel the way you do? Why is the gospel what you say it is?"

"First you need to reflect on your question about authority. In the Scriptures, whose question is it? And of whom is the answer required? Secondly, the gospel is not what I say it is. The gospel is the way of salvation proclaimed in the Scriptures."

"According to *your* interpretation, grace is mediated through faith alone. The interpretation of the Catholic church is different. Grace is mediated through the sacraments. How do you know that you are correct?"

"Let me answer your question with a question. When the Catholic church has decided upon a certain doctrinal issue, how is their decision brought to the people?"

"What do you mean?"

"How do the people learn of the decision, and how do they come to understand the content?"

"Through the teaching of the church."

"Encyclicals, bulls, sermons, decisions of ecumenical councils, and so forth?"

"Yes, that's right."

"But all these means have one thing in common. They all use language."

"Of course they do. But what's the problem?"

"Well, let's take the doctrine of papal infallibility. The church teaches that when he speaks *ex cathedra*, the pope is infallible. Is that right?"

"That is correct."

"But how does the average Catholic know that this is the real meaning? Why couldn't these words mean that the pope is infallible every second Tuesday?"

"Because that's not what the words *say*."

"So isn't it up to each individual Catholic to take these words honestly? I mean the magisterium cannot interpret itself, because then *that* interpretation could be equally distorted, and so on."

"Well, I guess so." Michael looked dubious.

"But if it is possible for individuals to approach the decrees of the church with an honest respect for language, why is it impossible to do the same with the Scriptures? They too were written in human language. There is no way to deny that a man can understand the Scriptures for himself without simultaneously denying that he can understand anything for himself—including the teaching of his interpreters."

"But when you challenge the teaching of the church, you are striking at the heart of the church. Without the magisterium, there is no Catholic church. Without the magisterium, you have doctrinal chaos. Every man does what is right in his own eyes."

"But what prevents every man from doing the same with the magisterium? Now I do not deny that the church could have a teaching office such as you describe. I am only saying that if it does, then that teaching office must be clearly set out in the Scriptures. We must not say that this teaching office exists because the church says it does. *That* is the point at issue. I am saying that the Scriptures must teach it, and that the Scriptures, like everything else that uses language, can be understood by the honest reader."

"But the Scriptures do give this authority to the church."

"According to the church. But what happens when we approach the Scriptures independently, without looking through the filter of the magisterium?"

"So what is the bottom line?"

"The bottom line is faith. Will you put your faith in the Scriptures—honestly understood—or will you put your faith in your church—honestly understood?"

Michael turned away. He still looked dubious.